Simply Charming *Circles*
Table of Contents

Pattern	Page Number
Introduction	1
Flowers for Sal	3
Flowers for Sal's Table	6
Raw Edge Sal	9
Sprinkles on Top	12
Machine Appliqué Templates	15
Raw Edge Appliqué Templates	20
Charming Windmills	21
Pinwheel Flowers	23
Charming Bulls Eye	26
Helter Skelter	29
Bonus Quilt #1: Baby Bulls Eye	31
Bonus Quilt #2: Charming Pinwheels	32
Appendix A: Bias Binding	33
Appendix B: Midge's Perfect Sashing and Borders	34
Appendix C: Piecing a Back	35

Moose on the Porch Quilts
Konda Luckau
665 E 400 S, Payson, UT 84651
801-465-9892
www.moosequilts.com

Introduction:

While writing the pattern book *Simply Charming*, I continued coming up with ideas for quilt patterns with charm squares. It turns out that I have not ended my love affair with charm packs. I love to pick up a charm pack and flip through it looking at the fabric, feeling the fabric, smelling the fabric and dreaming about making quilts from these little squares.

Though I don't appliqué, I couldn't help but think that charm squares were a fun size to make appliqué pieces. So I went with the circle -- the easiest shape to cut and appliqué. It is also very versatile. I also decided that if I wanted to make the quilts, the appliqué had to be simple. The patterns in this book use two very simple and fast methods of appliqué -- raw edge appliqué and machine appliqué. Even if you are as nervous about appliqué as I am, give these quilts a try. They aren't as intimidating as they sound.

Also, if you really like another method of appliqué, feel free to use what ever method you like on any of the quilts. Have fun!

Commonly Asked Questions about Charm Packs:

1) What is a charm pack?
A charm pack is a package of pre cut 5" squares. Generally a charm pack contains between 30 and 40 squares. All of the fabrics are different because the package includes one square of each fabric in a fabric line, excluding panels. Some fabric lines have one charm pack that contains the prints of the line and a separate charm pack that contains the woven fabrics which are commonly plaids of a particular line. Currently one fabric line puts two of each fabric in their charm packs making those quite a bit larger. Also, pre-measure your charm pack because currently one fabric line cuts their packs at $5\frac{1}{2}$" instead of the regular 5." This will not make a difference when making half square triangles, but it will make a difference when just using the squares.

2) Where can I buy charm packs?
Most quilt shops carry charm packs. They are also available online. Right now not all fabric manufacturers make charm packs, but more manufacturers will make them as everyone discovers how much fun they are!

3) What can I do with just one charm pack?
Some of the quilts in this book can be made with just one charm pack. Most of them can be made with just one charm pack if you forgo the charm square border. Depending on the size of the quilt you want to make and how many charms squares are in each package, you may want two or three charm packs.

4) What if my charm pack doesn't have enough squares in it?
Because the number of fabrics varies in each charm pack, it is impossible to tell the number of charm packs that each pattern will need. If a charm pack is lacking just a few squares, you have a couple options. First, you can always buy another charm pack and use the leftovers to make another quilt that doesn't take as many charms. Second, you can buy a fat quarter or two to get the extra fabric that you need. Another thing I have done, is purchase a little extra fabric for the borders or binding and cut a couple 5" squares out of the extra yardage.

5) Can I make these patterns without using charm packs?

Absolutely! Here are some places to find 5" squares:

~ Cut 5" squares out of your *scraps*. All of these quilt patterns make fabulous scrap quilts.

~ Cut 5" squares out of *yardage*. When purchasing yardage for 5" squares, 1/3 yard is a good amount to buy. That will give you two 5" strips with just 2" leftover. These 5" strips can each be cut into 8 squares so 1/3 yard of fabric will give you 16 charm squares.

~ Cut 5" squares out of a *fat quarter*. You can cut twelve 5" squares out of one fat quarter with a couple inches leftover.

~~~ All the patterns in this book are Fat Quarter Friendly!

6) Why should I buy a charm pack?

Here are my top ten reasons to buy charm packs:

1) They are just so fun!
2) To quickly achieve a scrappy look.
3) All the fabrics match.
4) You get a piece of an entire fabric line.
5) The squares are already cut.
6) To say, "Thank you!"
7) To say, "Happy Birthday!"
8) To say, "Merry Christmas."
9) They are quicker gifts than making cookies, less fattening, and last longer.
10) To be adventurous!

The reason I picked up my first charm pack was to be adventurous and stretch myself. I rarely buy plaids or grayed fabrics, but I love the comfortable look of quilts made using these fabrics. I decided to challenge myself to make a plaid quilt. I had a terrible time trying to select these fabrics. I fell in love with all the new brown fabrics that had come out, but I still couldn't get to the plaids. I wasn't brave enough to buy fabric I didn't absolutely love.

That was when I purchased a few of *Moda's Chocolat Wovens Charm Packs*. The result was *Simply Twisted,* which is in *Simply Charming,* and I was hooked! I love that quilt, and I never would have made it if I had to buy the fabrics one at a time. My hand would have passed over at least half of the fabrics.

For me, charm packs are mini-kits. Someone has put together 30-40 fabrics that look fabulous with each other. Occasionally in a charm pack, there are one or two fabrics that I really don't like. I will usually force myself to sew it into the quilt. Many times I find myself surprised that I like the offending fabric just fine once the quilt is finished because of the dimension and depth it adds to the quilt. Other times, I still don't like it, but there are only one or two in the quilt, so I am not disappointed with the overall result. And often I find that the fabric that I thought was so offensive is exactly the fabric that another person loves. That's part of the fun of quilting!

Good luck! I hope you have as much fun with these patterns as I have had making them.
Thanks, Konda Luckau

Flowers for Sal
67" x 80"
40 blocks
9½" block (9" finished)

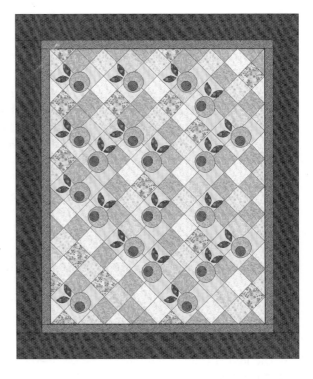

When I first designed this quilt, the flowers were blue and reminded me of blueberries. The blueberries reminded me of an old picture book that I have often read to my children, "Blueberries for Sal." That is why I named the quilt, "Flowers for Sal." Look for fabric for your flowers, flower centers, and leaves with good contrast with the rest of your fabric. In my quilt, the fabric I chose for the flowers ended up having only medium contrast because the fabric had such bold prints. You may want to look outside a specific fabric line to find the contrast you are looking for.

Because it is set "on point," the quilt has a tendency to stretch. There are instructions to stay-stitch the outer blocks to prevent this stretch. Also, because we are using charm squares and not special setting triangles, the points of the outside squares do get lost in the first border. Moda fabric is used in this quilt: Soirée by Lila Tueller.

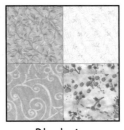

Block A
Make 20

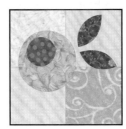

Block B
Make 20

Fabric Requirements:

160 charm (5") squares or 14 fat quarters
      or 1 layer cake
½ yard for flowers
⅛ yard for flower centers
¼ yard for leaves
⅔ yard for inner border
1⅔ yard for outer border
4 yards for backing (Method 2)
¾ yard for binding

1½ yard of 18" wide lightweight fusible webbing

Cutting Instructions:
1) From inner border fabric, cut 7 -- 2½" strips width of fabric.
    a) Cut one of these strips in half.
2) From outer border fabric, cut 8 -- 6½" strips width of fabric.

Sewing Instructions:
1) Take the 160 charm squares and make 40 four patch blocks as shown in **Figure A**. 20 of these blocks will be for the flowers. Press.

2) Take the fusible webbing. Lay it over the templates on page 15. Trace 20 copies of the 4 inch Circle Template on the fusible webbing. Following the manufacturer's instructions fuse the webbing onto the back of the flower fabric. Cut on the line. Peel the backing off the fusible webbing.

3) Take the fusible webbing. Lay it over the templates on page 15. Trace 20 copies of

Figure A
Make 40

the 2 inch Circle Template on the fusible webbing. Following the manufacturer's instructions fuse the webbing onto the back of the flower center fabric. Cut on the line. Peel the backing off the fusible webbing.

4) Take the fusible webbing. Lay it over the templates on page 15. Trace 40 copies of the Small Leaf Template on the fusible webbing. Following the manufacturer's instructions fuse the webbing onto the back of the leaf fabric. Cut on the line. Peel the backing off the fusible webbing.

5) Lay out 1 flower, 1 center, and 2 leaves on the 20 four patch blocks set aside for the flowers as shown in **Figure B: Placement Diagram**. Once the placement is correct, fuse according to manufacturer's instructions. Repeat with each of the 20 four patch blocks.

6) With a coordinating thread, stitch around the curved edge of the flower, the flower center, and each leaf with a blanket stitch, narrow zigzag, or with another decorative stitch.

7) With the remaining 20 four patch blocks, 12 will be used in the middle of the quilt. Set these aside.

8) The last 8 four patch blocks will be used as "setting triangles" around the edge of the quilt. Draw a diagonal line on the back of each block. Sew an $\frac{1}{8}$" on BOTH sides of the line through each block individually as shown in **Figure C**. This is a "stay-stitching" line. It will help prevent these blocks from stretching as the borders are sewn on. It will not be removed so the stitching needs to be less than the $\frac{1}{4}$" so it will not show.

Figure B: Placement Diagram

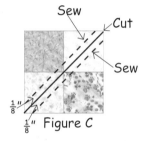

Figure C

9) Take one of those 8 four patch blocks to be used for the corners. Draw an additional diagonal line on the back of that block so it makes an "X." Sew an $\frac{1}{8}$" on BOTH sides of this line as well. Now cut on the lines of this block as well as the 7 other blocks.

10) Lay out the quilt as shown in **Figure D: Assembly Diagram** on page 5.

11) Assemble the center of the quilt together by sewing diagonal rows together. Match up the corners of the block.

12) Refer to Appendix B for instructions on sewing on border strips. Take 2 of the $2\frac{1}{2}$" inner border strips. Sew them together to make a long strip. Repeat with two more strips. Sew one of these strips onto the left side of the quilt and another one onto the right side of the quilt. Press.

13) Take the two half $2\frac{1}{2}$" inner border strips. Sew each one onto a whole strip. Sew one of these strips onto the top of the quilt and the other strip onto the bottom of the quilt. Press.

14) Take two of the $6\frac{1}{2}$" outer border strips. Sew them together. Repeat with the other 6 strips to make four double strips. First sew one of these strips onto the left side of the quilt. Sew another one onto the right side of the quilt. Press. Sew a third strip onto the top of the quilt. Sew the last strip onto the bottom of the quilt. Press.

15) Refer to Appendix C Method 2 to cut and sew the backing fabric.

16) Cut 8 -- $2\frac{1}{2}$" strips width of fabric for the binding.

Figure D: Assembly Diagram

Alternate Size Chart

	Baby Size	Throw	Twin Size	Queen Size
Dimensions	39½" x 52"	54" x 67"	67" x 80"	95" x 95"
Layout	2 x 3	3 x 4	4 x 5	5 x 5
Charm Squares	48	96	160	200
Flowers	6	12	20	25
1st Border	2", ⅜ yard	2", ½ yard	2", ⅔ yard	2", ¾ yard
2nd Border	5", 1 yard	6", 1¼ yard	6", 1⅔ yard	5", 1⅓ yards
3rd Border	none	none	none	8½", 2⅓ yards
Backing	1⅔ yards	3⅓ yards	4 yards	7 yards
Binding	½ yard	⅔ yard	¾ yard	1 yard

5

Flowers for Sal's Table
37" x 37"
4 blocks
$9\frac{1}{2}$" block (9" finished)

This sweet table topper (or wall hanging or baby quilt) uses the same flower as the previous quilt "Flowers for Sal." The leaves are placed differently on the blocks in relation to the flowers. This is because of the difference in placing the blocks on point or straight.

Fabric Requirements:
23 charm (5") squares
      16 for background
      4 for flowers
      1 for flower centers
      2 for leaves
$\frac{1}{2}$ yard for sashing
1 yard for outer border
$1\frac{1}{4}$ yards for backing
$\frac{1}{2}$ yard for binding

$\frac{1}{3}$ yard of 18" wide lightweight fusible webbing

Cutting Instructions:
1) Cut sashing and inner border fabric into the following strips:
    a) Cut 4 -- $2\frac{1}{2}$" strips width of fabric:
        A) Take one of these strips and cut it into 4 -- $2\frac{1}{2}$" x $9\frac{1}{2}$"
        B) Take another strip and cut it into 2 -- $2\frac{1}{2}$" x $20\frac{1}{2}$"
        C) Take the last two strips and cut them each to $2\frac{1}{2}$" x $24\frac{1}{2}$"
2) Cut outer border fabric into 4 -- $7\frac{1}{2}$" strips width of fabric.
    a) Cut two of these $7\frac{1}{2}$" x $24\frac{1}{2}$"
    b) Cut the other two $7\frac{1}{2}$" x $38\frac{1}{2}$"
    c) Take one of the scraps and cut one $2\frac{1}{2}$" square for the square in the center of the quilt.
3) Cut the fusible webbing into 7 -- $4\frac{1}{2}$" squares.

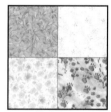

Figure A

Sewing Instructions:
1) Take the 16 -- 5" background squares and sew them into 4 four patch blocks as shown in **Figure A**. Press.

2) Following the manufacturers instructions, fuse the lightweight fusible webbing onto the BACK of the remaining 7 charm squares.

3) Take the lightweight cardboard that came with one of the charm squares or other template material and make a copy of the 4 inch Circle Template on page 15. Trace the 4 inch Circle on the back of the 4 flower squares.

4) Take another piece of cardboard and make a copy of the 2 inch Circle Template and the Small Leaf Template also on page 15. Trace 4 -- 2" circles on the back of the flower center

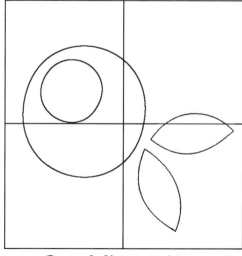

Figure B: Placement Diagram

charm square. Trace 4 leaves on each leaf charm square making a total of 8 leaves. Cut out all of these circles and leaves on the lines and peel off the backing of the fusible webbing.

5) Lay out 1 flower, 1 center, and 2 leaves on each of the four patch blocks as shown in **Figure B: Placement Diagram** on the previous page. Once the placement is correct, fuse according to manufacturers instructions. Repeat with each of the 4 four patch blocks.

6) With a coordinating thread, stitch around the curved edge of the flower, the flower center, and each leaf with a blanket stitch, narrow zigzag, or with another decorative stitch.

7) Lay out quilt as shown in **Figure C: Assembly Diagram**, turning the flower blocks so they are arranged in a pleasing manner. Using the 4 flower blocks, the 4 -- $2\frac{1}{2}$" x $9\frac{1}{2}$" sashing strips, and the $2\frac{1}{2}$" center square, assemble the three rows as shown in Figure C. Press seam allowances toward the sashing strip.

8) Sew the rows together to assemble the quilt center. The quilt should now measure $20\frac{1}{2}$" x $20\frac{1}{2}$."

9) Take the 2 -- $2\frac{1}{2}$" x $20\frac{1}{2}$" inner border strips. Sew one of them onto the left side of the quilt. Sew the other one onto the right side of the quilt. Press.

10) Take the 2 -- $2\frac{1}{2}$" x $24\frac{1}{2}$" inner border strips. Sew one of them onto the top of the quilt. Sew the other one onto the bottom of the quilt. Press.

11) Take the 2 -- $7\frac{1}{2}$" x $24\frac{1}{2}$" inner border strips. Sew them onto the left side and the right side of the quilt. Press.

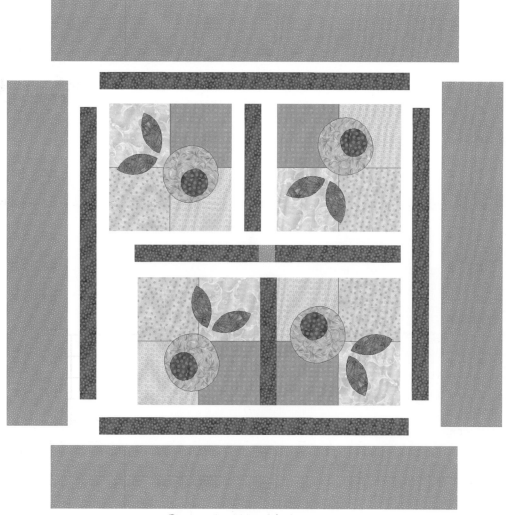

Figure C: Assembly Diagram

12) Take the 2 -- 7½" x 38½" inner border strips. Sew them onto the top and the bottom of the quilt. Press. Using the scallop template, mark the scallop on the edge of the outer border as shown in **Figure D: Scallop Placement Diagram**. DO NOT cut the scallop until the quilt is quilted.

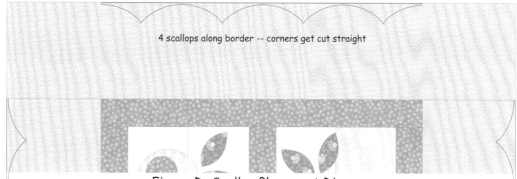

4 scallops along border -- corners get cut straight

Figure D: Scallop Placement Diagram

13) Using the ½ yard of binding fabric, cut 2½" BIAS strips for the binding and join these strips together as shown in Appendix A: Bias Binding on page 33.

14) AFTER the quilt is quilted, cut along the scalloped edge. Sew the binding onto the right side of the quilt.

15) Tips for binding a scallop:

- Start and end on the straightest possible part.
- Stop when you get directly below the lowest point as shown in Figure F.
- With needle down, rotate fabric and stretch out scallop. Take a couple stitches and stop with needle down.
- Rotate fabric and sew the next scallop.
- When binding is sewn on, clip each inside curve as shown in Figure F. Be Careful NOT to clip the seam.

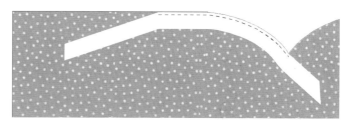

Figure E

16) Finish the binding by hand on the back of the quilt. Following the tips above, the binding will lay nice and neat on the front and the back.

clip

Figure F

Alternate Size Chart

	Baby Size	Throw	Twin Size	Queen Size
Dimensions	37" x 37"	49" x 60"	60" x 82"	95" x 95"
Layout	2 x 2	3 x 4	4 x 6	6 x 6
Charm Squares	23	69	138	207
Sashing/1st Border	½ yard	1 yard	1⅓ yards	1¾ yards
2nd Border	7", 1 yard	7", 1⅓ yards	7", 1⅔ yard	5", 1¼ yards
3rd Border	none	none	none	8½", 2⅓ yards
Backing	1¼ yards	2¼ yards	3½ yards	7 yards
Binding	½ yard	½ yard	⅔ yard	1 yard

Raw Edge Sal
62" x 89"
15 blocks
14" block (13½" finished)

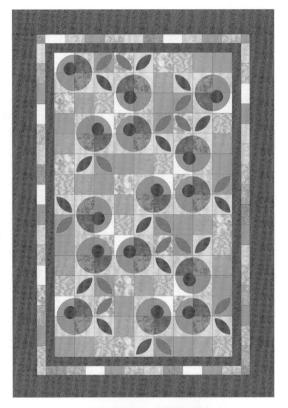

I was having so much fun with different layout of *Flowers for Sal* that I thought I would combine the raw edge technique from the other quilts in this book to make a raw edge flower quilt similar to *Flowers for Sal*. Most of the fabric in this quilt is from Clothworks' Cherry Blossom fabric line by Chris Chun. Where the seams intersect underneath the flower center may cause the flower center to wear quicker than normal. I have included instructions to place a piece of flannel underneath the flower center. This should protect the flower center from unusual wear.

Fabric Requirements:
> 75 charm (5") squares or 7 fat quarters
>> 60 for flowers
>> 15 for leaves
>
> 14 fat quarters for the background
>> --or-- 162 more charm (5") squares
>
> ¼ yard fabric for flower centers
>> --or--1 fat quarter or 15 charm squares
>
> ¼ yard flannel that coordinates with flower centers
> 2¼ yards for the inner and outer borders
> 5 yards fabric for backing (Method 3)
> ⅔ yard fabric for binding

Materials Needed:
> Ruler for cutting circles (optional)
>> Easy Circle Cut Ruler
>> Cut a Round Tool (Standard or Midi)

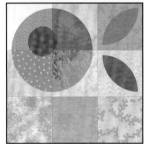

Make 15

Cutting Instructions:
1) Cut 14 background fat quarters into 162 -- 5" squares.
> a) Take 27 of these 5" background squares and cut them in half so they measure 2½" x 5."
> b) Take 2 of the 2½" x 5" rectangles and cut them in half to make 4 --2½" squares.

2) Cut border fabric into the following width of fabric:
> a) Cut 7 -- 2¾" strips.
>> A) Cut one of these in half.
> b) Cut 8 -- 7" strips.

Sewing Instructions:
1) Take the lightweight cardboard that came with one of the charm squares and make a copy of the Large Charm Square Quarter Circle Template, on page 20.

2) Use this template with the 60 flower 5" charm squares. Align the two straight edges of the template along two straight edges of each charm square. Trace the template onto the back of all 60 flower 5" charm squares. Cut on the line. This can also be done using the Easy Cut Circle Ruler or the Cut a Round Tool.

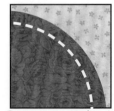

Figure A: Make 60

3) Place each of these quarter circles on a 5" background square so that the corners of the quarter circles match the corners of the 5" background square as shown in **Figure A** on the previous page. This is done with the right sides of BOTH fabrics facing upwards. Pin in place.

Figure B: Make 30

4) Now sew the quarter circle to the 5" background square. These are sewn with a raw edge appliqué technique which means that the seam allowance of the appliquéd piece is on the outside and is intended to fray. Sew along the curved edge with a ½" seam. Sew down all 60 large quarter circles in the same manner.

5) Take a second piece of cardboard and make a copy of the Large Leaf Template on page 20.

6) Use the Leaf Template with the 15 leaf 5" squares. Trace TWO Leaf Templates onto each 5" leaf square. Cut out on the line. Center each leaf on a 5" background square as shown in **Figure B**. Pin in place. Sew along the curved edge with a ½" seam in the same manner as the flower squares. Repeat to make 30 leaf squares.

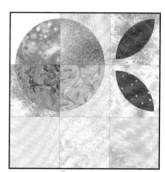
Figure C

7) Take 4 flower squares, 2 leaf squares and 3 plain background squares to make one block as shown in Figure C. Make 15 of these blocks. Press.

8) Make a copy of the Flower Center Template on page 20. Trace 15 flower centers on the back of the flower center fabric. Cut on the line. Repeat with the flannel to make 15 flannel flower centers.

9) Use one Flower Center and one Flannel Flower Center for each block. Place flower center on top of flannel flower center with both fabrics right sides up. Position double flower center as shown in Figure D. Sew along the edge with a ½" seam. Repeat with all 15 blocks.

10) Layout quilt center as shown in **Figure E: Assembly Diagram** on page 11.

11) Sew blocks into rows. Press. Sew rows together to complete quilt center. The quilt should now measure 41" x 68."

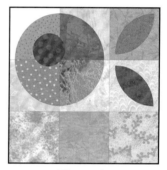
Figure D

12) Take the 2¾" border strips. Sew each of the half strips onto a whole strip. Take two whole 2¾" strips and sew them together. Repeat with the last two 2¾" strips. Refer to Appendix B on page 34 for tips on sewing on borders.

13) Take the two double 2¾" strips. Sew one onto the left side of the quilt. Sew the other onto the right side of the quilt. Take the other two long 2¾" strips. Sew one onto the top of the quilt and sew the other one on the bottom of the quilt. Press.

14) Layout the pieced border using the 2½" x 5" rectangles and the 2½" corner squares. There are 10 rectangles that make up the top and bottom borders and 16 rectangles that make up the left and right borders. Sew the corner squares onto the top and bottom borders.

15) First sew on the left and right pieced borders. Then sew on the top and bottom pieced borders.

16) Take the 7" border strips. Take two whole 7" strips and sew them together. Repeat with the rest making 4 double 7" strips.

17) Take one double 7" strips. Sew it onto the left side of the quilt. Sew a second one onto the right side of the quilt. Sew a third one onto the top of the quilt and sew the last 7" strip onto the bottom of the quilt.

18) Refer to Appendix C Method 3 to cut and sew the backing fabric.

19) Cut 8 -- 2½" strips width of fabric for the binding.

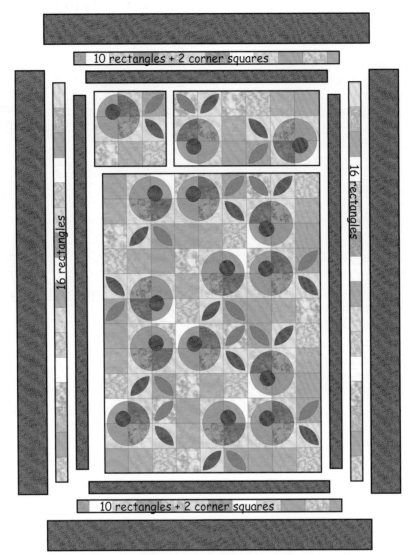

Figure E: Assembly Diagram

Alternate Size Chart

	Baby Size	Throw	Twin Size	Queen Size
Dimensions	43" x 43"	62" x 62"	62" x 89"	95" x 95"
Layout	2 x 2	3 x 3	3 x 5	5 x 5
Flower Fat Quarters	2	3	5	9
Flower Center FQ	1	1	1	1
Leaf FQ	1	1	1	1
Bkgrd/2nd Border FQ	5	9	14	22
1st/3rd Borders	$2\frac{1}{4}$",$3\frac{1}{2}$"--1 yard	$2\frac{1}{4}$",$6\frac{1}{2}$"--1 yard	$2\frac{1}{4}$",$6\frac{1}{2}$"--$2\frac{1}{4}$ yards	$2\frac{1}{4}$", $9\frac{1}{2}$"--$3\frac{1}{4}$ yards
Backing	2 yards	4 yards	5 yards	7 yards
Binding	$\frac{1}{2}$ yard	$\frac{2}{3}$ yard	$\frac{2}{3}$ yard	1 yard

Flowers for Sal
Pieced by Karlene Riggs
Quilted by Konda Luckau

Raw Edge Sal
Pieced by Michelle Hansen
Quilted by Konda Luckau

Flowers for Sal's Table
Pieced by Konda Luckau
Quilted by Konda Luckau

Charming Bulls Eye
Pieced by April Mazzoleni
Quilted by Konda Luckau

Charming Windmills
Pieced by Konda Luckau
Quilted by Konda Luckau

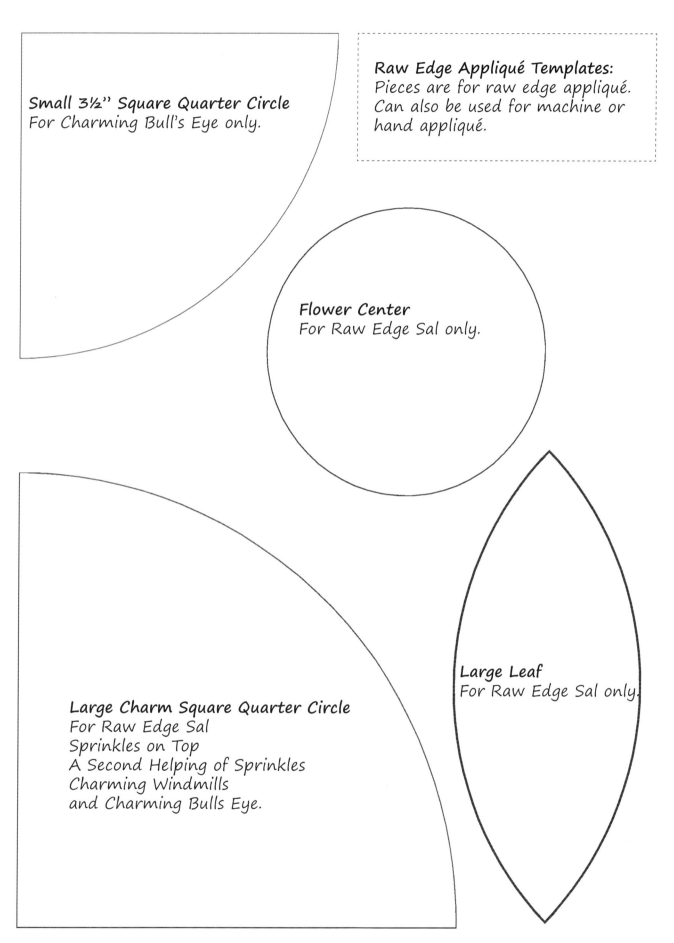

Small 3½" Square Quarter Circle
For Charming Bull's Eye only.

Raw Edge Appliqué Templates:
Pieces are for raw edge appliqué. Can also be used for machine or hand appliqué.

Flower Center
For Raw Edge Sal only.

Large Charm Square Quarter Circle
For Raw Edge Sal
Sprinkles on Top
A Second Helping of Sprinkles
Charming Windmills
and Charming Bulls Eye.

Large Leaf
For Raw Edge Sal only.

Charming Windmills
65" x 83"
35 blocks
$9\frac{1}{2}$" block (9" finished)

This quilt was inspired by a traditional quilt, the Hunter's Star. I added curves and made it raw edge instead of pieced so it is very different than the original, but still has the same light and dark affect as the Hunter's Star. Moda fabrics were used in this quilt: Portobello Market by 3 Sisters. Not only do I love this fabric line, but it's name also reminds me of the song "Portobello Road" from the old movie "Bedknobs and Broomsticks." So I am always singing when I sew with this fabric. The quilt works so well with 1 layer cake and 2 charm packs that I have not included instructions for resizing this quilt.

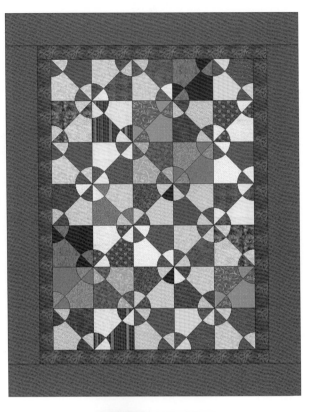

Fabric Requirements:
> 1 layer cake (or 9 -- ⅓ yard pieces)
> 72 charm (5") squares (or 6 fat quarters)
> > ideally there should be
> > 2 of each charm square
> 1 yard fabric for the inner border
> 2 yards fabric for outer border
> 5 yards fabric for backing (Method 3)
> ¾ yard fabric for binding

Materials Needed:
> $9\frac{1}{2}$" Square Ruler (or larger)
> Ruler for cutting circles (optional)
> > Easy Circle Cut Ruler
> > Cut a Round Tool (Standard or Midi)

Make 36

Cutting Instructions:
1) If using ⅓ yard pieces and fat quarters, cut the ⅓ yard pieces each into 4 -- 10" squares giving a total of 36 -- 10" squares. Cut the fat quarters each into 12 -- 5" squares giving a total of 72 -- 5" squares.
2) Cut the inner border fabric into 7 -- $3\frac{1}{2}$" strips width of fabric.
> a) Cut one of these in half.
3) Cut the outer border fabric into 8 -- $7\frac{1}{2}$" strips width of fabric.

Sewing Instructions:
1) Take the lightweight cardboard square that came with one of the charm squares or other template material and make a copy of the Large Charm Square Quarter Circle, on page 20.

2) Use this template with the 72 -- 5" charm squares. Align the two straight edges of the template along two straight edges of each charm square. Trace the template onto the back of all 72 -- 5" charm squares. Cut on the line. This can also be done using the Easy Circle Cut Ruler or the Cut a Round Tool.

3) Match up the 2 charm squares and the layer cake that are identical so there are 36 sets. (If they don't match up exactly, match up so they are similar.) Now, there may be some concern that we have 36 sets when there are 35 blocks. It needs to be this way because the blocks are made in pairs. There will be one leftover block. It would make a great label on the back of your quilt if you so choose.

4) Separate the sets into 18 light sets and 18 dark sets. If there are some fabrics that are of medium value, just assign them to be either light or dark. That isn't a problem.

5) Now pair up one "light" fabric set with one "dark" fabric set. For the medium value fabrics just try to pick fabrics that are "light" and "dark" relative to each other. For example, if the "light" set selected

isn't very light then placing it with a "dark" fabric set that is really dark will make the light fabric seem light because it is definitely lighter than the fabric that it is paired with.

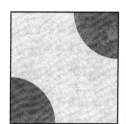
Figure A: Make 18

Figure B: Make 18

6) Once the fabrics are all paired up, swap the 10″ squares so that the 2 light 4½″ quarter circles are with the dark 10″ square and the 2 dark 4½″ quarter circles are with the light 10″ square. Place the quarter circles in opposite corners so that the corners of the quarter circles match the corners of the 10″ square as shown in **Figures A and B**. This is done with the right sides of BOTH fabrics facing upwards. Pin in place. We will need these squares to still be paired up in step 9 so don't let these lose track of each other.

7) Now sew all of the quarter circles to the 10″ square they have been placed on. These are assembled with a raw edge appliqué technique. Sew along the curved edge with a ½″ seam.

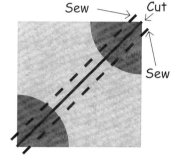
Figure C

8) Sew down all of the quarter circles in the same manner so each 10″ square has 2 quarter circles sewn onto it in opposite corners. Trim the seam allowance behind the quarter circle to about a ¼.″

9) Draw a diagonal line on the BACK of all of the LIGHT 10″ squares so that the line goes THROUGH each of the quarter circles. Place one of the 10″ squares and its pair with RIGHT sides together and with the quarter circles together. Sew a **scant** ¼″ on both sides of the diagonal line as shown in **Figure C**.

10) Cut ON the diagonal line. Press seam allowance toward the dark square.

11) Take 9½″ (or larger) square ruler and square up each block to 9½.″

12) Layout the quilt as shown in **Figure D**. Assemble the center of the quilt. Press these seam allowances to the light square. The seams where the circle matches up should all be laying nicely either clockwise or counter clockwise. You can open up the intersection to help it lay down a little flatter. The center of the quilt should now measure 45½″ x 63½.″

13) Refer to Appendix B on page 34 for instructions on sewing borders. Take two of the 3½″ inner border strips. Sew them together. Repeat with the last two strips. Sew these strips onto the left side and the right side of the quilt .

14) Take the 3½″ inner border strips. Sew each half strip onto a whole strip. Sew these strips onto the top and the bottom of the quilt.

15) Take two of the 7½″ inner border strips. Sew them together. Repeat with the other 6 strips so there are 4 long strips. First sew one of these strips onto the left side of the quilt and another to the right side of the quilt. Then sew one of these strips onto the top of the quilt and the last strip onto the bottom of the quilt.

16) Refer to Appendix C Method 3 to cut and sew the backing fabric.

17) Cut 8 -- 2½″ strips width of fabric for the binding.

Figure D: Assembly Diagram

Pinwheel Flowers
66" x 91"
15 blocks
11" block (10½" finished)

This quilt came about as I was playing with the idea of making curved pinwheels. I came up with several ways to do it, but I ended up with machine appliqué. I really like the result. I actually sewed my finger while longarm quilting a 3-D pinwheel quilt so I like that these are stuck down. This quilt was made with Moda Fabric: Crazy Eights by Sandy Gervais.

Fabric Requirements:
  92 charm (5") squares or 8 fat quarters
    32 dark squares for backgrounds
    14 dark squares for flowers
    28 light squares for backgrounds
    16 light squares for flowers
    2 for sashing posts
1¼ yards for sashing
¾ yard for first border
1¼ yards for second border and block centers
2¼ yards for third border
5 yards for backing (Method 3)
¾ yard for binding

1¼ yards of 18" wide fusible webbing

Cutting Instructions:
1) Cut the sashing fabric into the following strips width of fabric:
  a) Cut into 8 -- 2" strips:
    A) Cut strips into 60 -- 2" x 5" rectangles.
  b) Cut into 8 -- 2½" strips:
    A) Cut strips into 22 -- 2½" x 11" rectangles.
2) Cut the first border fabric into 7 -- 2½" strips width of fabric.
  a) Cut one of these strips in half.
3) Cut the second border fabric into the following strips width of fabric:.
  a) Cut 7 -- 5" strips.
    A) Cut one of these strips in half.
  b) Cut 1 -- 2" strips.
    A) Cut 15 -- 2" squares for flower centers.
4) Cut the third border fabric into 8 -- 9" strips width of fabric.
5) Cut the two 5" charm squares into a total of 8 -- 2½" squares for the cornerstones.
6) Cut fusible webbing into 30 -- 4½" squares.

Make 8

Sewing Instructions:

1) Separate 5" charm squares into 46 dark squares and 44 light squares. Take 16 of the light squares and 14 of the dark squares to be used as flowers. Following the manufacturers instructions, fuse the webbing onto the BACK of these 30 flower squares.

2) Using the lightweight cardboard that came with the charm squares or other tem-

Make 7

plate material, make a copy of the 4 inch Circle Template on page 15. Trace a 4 inch circle on the back of the 30 flower circles. Cut on the lines. Fold circles in half and finger press. Open and cut on the fold so there are 60 half circles.

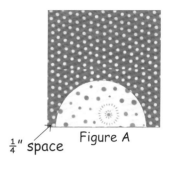

3) Take the 32 dark 5" squares and the 32 light half circles. Place each light half circle on a dark square along one edge with a $\frac{1}{4}$" space as shown in **Figure A**. Press the circle in place. Repeat to make 32 dark blocks.

$\frac{1}{4}$" space   Figure A

4) Take the 28 light 5" squares and the 28 dark half circles. Repeat the previous step to make 28 light blocks.

5) Take all 60 flower squares and topstitch, with a coordinating thread, around the curved edge with a blanket stitch, narrow zigzag, or with another decorative stitch.

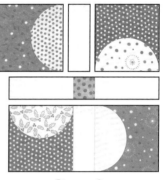

6) Take four of the dark squares (with light flowers), four 2" x 5" inner sashing strips and one 2" flower center square and sew a dark block together as shown in **Figure B**. Repeat to make 8 dark blocks.

7) Take four of the light squares (with dark flowers), four 2" x 5" inner sashing strips and one 2" flower center square and sew a light block together in the same manner as the dark blocks. Repeat to make 7 light blocks.

Figure B

8) Take 12 of the 2$\frac{1}{2}$" x 11" sashing rectangles and the 8 -- 2$\frac{1}{2}$" cornerstone squares. Sew together 4 strips as shown in **Figure C**. Press towards cornerstones.

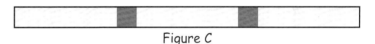

Figure C

9) Layout the quilt as shown below in **Figure D: Assembly Diagram** on page 25.

10) Take the 2$\frac{1}{2}$" x 11" rectangles and sew one on each side of the center block in each row. Sew first and last blocks onto the center sashed block to complete each row. Press towards sashing strips.

11) Sew the rows together to make quilt center. The quilt center should measure 48" x 67."

12) Refer to Appendix B for instructions on sewing border strips. Sew together two 2$\frac{1}{2}$" first border strips. Repeat with two more strips. Sew these onto the left side and the right side of the quilt. Press.

13) Take the two half 2$\frac{1}{2}$" first border strips. Sew each one onto a whole strip. Sew these onto the top and the bottom of the quilt. Press.

14) Sew together two of the 5" second border strips. Repeat with two more strips. Sew one of these onto the left side and the other onto the right side of the quilt. Press.

15) Take the two half 5" second border strips. Sew each one of them onto a whole strip. Sew these onto the top and the bottom of the quilt. Press.

16) Sew together two of the 9" third border strips. Repeat to make four double strips. Sew one of these onto the left side and another onto the right side of the quilt. Press. Sew a third strip onto the top of the quilt and the last strip onto the bottom of the quilt.

17) Refer to Appendix C Method 3 to cut and sew the backing fabric.

18) Cut 9 -- 2$\frac{1}{2}$" strips width of fabric for the binding.

Figure D: Assembly Diagram

Alternate Size Chart

	Baby Size	Throw	Twin Size	Queen Size
Dimensions	39" x 39"	52" x 64"	66" x 91"	91" x 91"
Layout	2 x 2	3 x 4	3 x 5	5 x 5
Charm Squares	25	74	92	154
Sashing	⅓ yard	1 yard	1¼ yards	2 yards
1st Border	2", ½ yard	2", ½ yard	2", ⅔ yard	2", ¾ yard
2nd Border	6", 1 yard	6", 1¼ yards	4½", 1¼ yards	4½", 1½ yards
3rd Border	none	none	8½", 2¼ yards	8½", 2½ yards
Backing	1¼ yards	3⅓ yards	5 yards	7 yards
Binding	½ yard	⅔ yard	¾ yard	1 yard

Charming Bulls Eye
73" x 86"
80 blocks
7" block (6½" finished)

This quilt inspired this whole book. Many years ago I bought the pattern to make the traditional bulls eye quilt. I selected my fabric and cut it into squares and then I put it away. I couldn't talk myself into cutting ALL those circles. Then one day I realized that I didn't have to make the whole circle. I could use a charm pack and cut a quarter circle! AND I could even get a ruler so I could cut it with a rotary cutter! Now I had a quilt that I could make. The quarter circle is such a gentle curve that it almost doesn't even need pinning. It is easy to cut and easy to sew. I hope this quilt will be your favorite like it is mine.

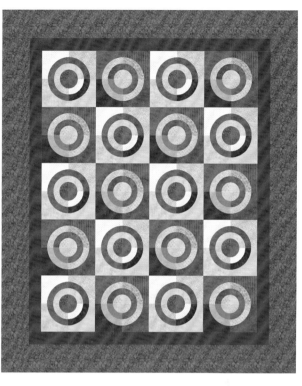

Fabric Requirements:
  20 fat quarters (or ¼ yard cuts)
      10 light colors
      10 dark colors
  80 charm (5") squares
  1 yard for inner border
  2 yards for outer border
  5½ yards backing (Method 3)
  ¾ yard binding

Materials Needed:
  Ruler for cutting circles (optional)
      Easy Circle Cut Ruler
      Cut a Round Tool (Standard or Midi)

Block A:
Make 40

Block B:
Make 40

Cutting Instructions:
1) Cut fat quarters (or ¼ yard cuts) into 4 -- 7" squares and 4 -- 3½" squares as shown at right.
2) Cut from inner border fabric 7 -- 3½" strips width of fabric.
    a) Cut one of these strips in half.
3) Cut from outer border fabric 8 -- 8" strips width of fabric.

3½"	3½"	3½"	3½"
7"		7"	
7"		7"	

Cutting for
Fat Quarter

Sewing Instructions:

1) Organize each size of fabric 7," 5," and 3½" into two piles, a light pile and a dark pile. These piles need to be evenly divided with 40 fabrics in each pile. If there is a fabric that you have a question about whether it is dark or light, just assign it to a pile. Medium value fabrics work just fine in this quilt.

2) Take the lightweight cardboard that came with one of the charm squares or other material and make a copy of the Large Charm Square Quarter Circle template, on page 20. Take another cardboard square and make a copy of the Small 3½" Square Quarter Circle template, also on page 20.

3) Use the Large Template with the 80 -- 5" charm squares. Align the two straight edges of the template along two straight edges of each charm square. Trace the Large Template onto the back of all 80 -- 5" charm squares. Cut on the line. This can also be done with the Easy Circle Cut Ruler or the Cut a

Round Tool.

4) Use the Small Template with the 80 -- 3½" squares. Trace this template onto the back of all 80 -- 3½" squares. Cut on the line. This can also be done using the Easy Cut Circle Ruler or the Cut a Round Tool.

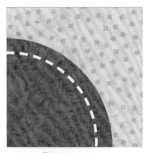

Figure A

5) Take the light pile of 7" squares, the dark pile of 5" quarter circles and the light pile of 3½" quarter circles. Now complete Steps 6 through 11 using these fabrics to make 40 of Block A.

6) Place the large quarter circles on the 7" square so that the corners of the quarter circles match the corners of the 7" square as shown in **Figure A**. This is done with the right sides of BOTH fabrics facing upwards. Pin in place.

7) Now sew the quarter circle to the 7" square. This is sewn with a raw edge appliqué technique which means that the seam allowance of the appliquéd piece is on the outside and is intended to fray. Sew along the curved edge with a ½" **seam**. Sew down all 40 of the large quarter circles in the same manner.

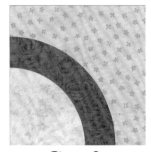

Figure B

8) Place one of the small 3½" quarter circles on a 7" square so that the corner of the small quarter circles matches the corner of the large quarter circle as shown in **Figure B**. This is done with the right sides of all the fabrics facing upwards. Pin in place.

9) Sew down the small quarter circles in the same way as the previous quarter circle. Sew along the curved edge with a ½" **seam**. Sew down all 40 of the small quarter circles in the same manner.

10) Trim *both the dark charm square quarter circle and the light background BEHIND the 3½" quarter circle* to about a ½". Don't worry about if your seam allowance is exact, but do try to cut it in a smooth curve. Repeat with all 40 blocks.

Figure C

11) Take these mini quarter circles that have been trimmed away and sew them on top of the small quarter circle as shown in **Figure C** in the same manner as the two previous quarter circles. Repeat with all 40 blocks.

12) Repeat steps 6 through 11 with the dark pile of 7" squares, the light pile of 5" quarter circles and the dark pile of 3½" quarter circles to make 40 of Block B.

13) Layout quilt center as shown in **Figure D: Assembly Diagram** on page 28. Sew blocks into rows using a ¼" seam. Press. Sew the rows together using a ¼" **seam** to finish assembling the quilt center. Press. The quilt should now measure 52½" x 65½."

14) Take two of the 3½" inner border strips. Sew them together. Repeat with the last two strips. Sew one of these strips onto the left side of the quilt. Sew the other one onto the right side of the quilt.

15) Take the remaining 3½" inner border strips. Sew each half strip onto a whole strip. Sew one of these strips onto the top of the quilt. Sew the other one onto the bottom of the quilt.

16) Sew together two of the 8" outer border strips. Repeat to make four double strips. Sew one of these onto the left side and another onto the right side of the quilt. Press. Sew a third strip onto the top of the quilt and the last strip onto the bottom of the quilt.

18) Refer to Appendix C Method 3 to cut and sew the backing fabric.

19) Cut 8 -- 2½" strips width of fabric for the binding.

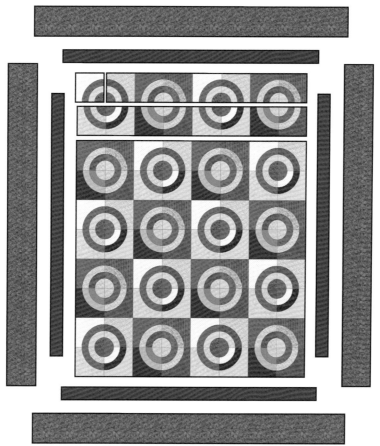

Figure D: Assembly Diagram

Alternate Size Chart

	Baby Size	Throw	Twin Size	Queen Size
Dimensions	40" x 40"	60" x 60"	73" x 86"	99" x 99"
Layout	4 x 4	6 x 6	8 x 10	12 x 12
Bkgrnd Fat Quarters	4	9	20	36
Charm Squares	16	36	80	144
1st Border	2", ⅓ yard	3", ⅔ yard	3", 1 yard	3", 1 yard
2nd Border	5", ⅔ yard	7½", 1½ yards	7½", 2 yards	7½", 2½ yards
Backing	1¼ yards	3 yards	5½ yards	7½ yards
Binding	½ yard	⅔ yard	¾ yard	1 yard

Helter Skelter
68" x 87"
35 blocks
10" block (9½" finished)

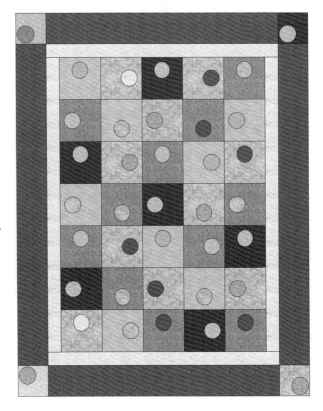

Helter Skelter came about as I was playing with a layer cake and a charm pack. I placed the circle off center and rotated the block so it looked a little funky. I really like the result. My first quilt I made with Moda's Dandelion Girl. While I did like that quilt a lot, my friend made her version in black and white and bright scraps, and I think it fits the contemporary feel of this pattern. The quilt works so well with 1 layer cake and 2 charm packs that I have not included instructions for resizing this quilt.

Fabric Requirements:
1 layer cake
  --or-- ten ⅓ yd, cut into 40 -- 10" squares
39 charm (5") squares
1 yard for inner border
1¾ yard for outer border
5 yards for backing (Method 3)
¾ yard for binding

1¼ yards of 18" wide fusible webbing

Cutting Instructions:
1) Cut fusible webbing into 39 -- 4½" squares.
2) Cut the inner border fabric into 7 -- 3½" strips width of fabric.
   a) Cut one of these strips in half.
3) Cut the outer border fabric into 7 -- 7½" strips width of fabric.
   a) Cut one of these strips in half.

Sewing Instructions:

1) Following the manufacturers instructions, fuse the lightweight fusible webbing onto the BACK of the 39 charm squares.

2) Using the lightweight cardboard from the charm squares or other material, make a copy of the 4 inch Circle Templates on page 15. Trace this circle on the back of all the 39 charm squares. Cut on the line. Peel off the backing of the fusible webbing.

3) Take four of the 10" squares and four of the circles to use for the corner blocks. Trim the squares to 7½" x 7½." Fold these squares in half and in half again and finger press the center. Open up the square and place the circle in the corner of the square so one edge is just over the center as shown in **Figure A**. Press the circle into place. Repeat to make 4 Corner Blocks. With a coordinating thread color, topstitch along the edge of each circle with a narrow zigzag or another decorative stitch.

4) Take one circle and one 10" square. Fold the 10" square in half and in half

Placement Lines

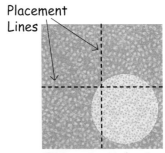

Figure A: Make 4 Corner Blocks

Placement Lines

Figure B: Make 35 Center Blocks

29

again to find the center. Finger press the center point. Open up the square and place the circle so one edge is at the center of the square as shown in **Figure B**. Press the circle into place. Repeat to make 35 Center Blocks. Topstitch these circles in the same manner as the other circles.

5) Layout the quilt as shown below in **Figure C: Assembly Diagram**. Sew quilt center together. The quilt center should measure 48" x 67."

6) Refer to Appendix B for instructions on sewing border strips. Sew together two 3½" inner border strips. Repeat with two more strips. Sew these onto the left side and the right side of the quilt. Press.

7) Take the two half 3½" inner border strips. Sew each one onto a whole strip. Sew these onto the top and the bottom of the quilt. Press.

8) Sew together two of the 7½" outer border strips. Repeat with two more strips. Sew one of these onto the left side and the other onto the right side of the quilt. Press.

9) Take the two half 7½" outer border strips. Sew each one of them onto a whole strip. Cut these two strips to 7½" x 54." Sew the two corner blocks onto one of these 7½" x 54" strips as shown in **Figure C: Assembly Diagram**. Pin and sew onto the top of the quilt. Sew on the bottom corner blocks to the other 7½" x 54" strip. Pin and sew onto the bottom of the quilt. Press.

10) Refer to Appendix C Method 3 to cut and sew the backing fabric.

11) Cut 8 -- 2½" strips width of fabric for the binding.

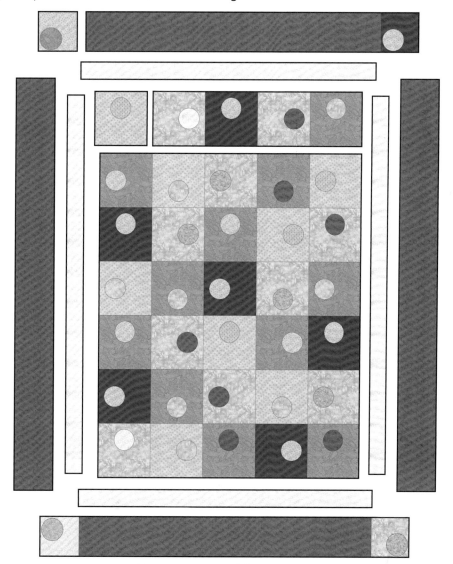

Figure C: Assembly Diagram

Bonus Quilt #1:
Baby Bulls Eye
(from extra of Charming Windmills)
50" x 50"
64 Blocks
5" block (4½" finished)

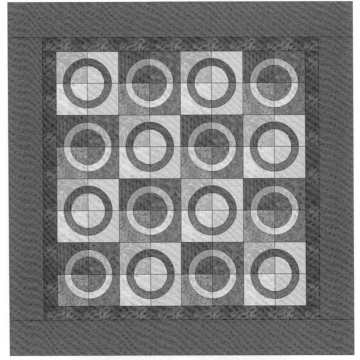

While not a true bonus quilt, this is pretty close. This quilt takes advantage of the quarter circle cut away from behind the block of the Charming Windmills quilt. Sew each of those onto a charm square and you have the starting of a bull's eye quilt.

Fabric Requirements:

64 of the quarter circles cut away from behind the block of the Charming Windmills quilt. (To make this quilt without making the Charming Windmills quilt, take 64 charm squares and cut them into quarter circles using the Large Charm Square Quarter Circle template on page 20.)

64 charm (5") squares
½ yard for inner border
1 yard for outer border
2¼ yards for backing (Method 1)
½ yard for binding

Block A:
Make 40

Block B:
Make 40

Cutting Instructions:

1) From the inner borders fabric cut 4 -- 2½" strips width of fabric.
2) From outer border fabric, cut 5 -- 5½" strips width of fabric
    a) Cut one of these strips in half.

Sewing Instructions:

1) Take the 64 cut away quarter circles and sew each of them onto a charm square with both fabrics right sides facing up as shown in **Figure A** with a ½" seam allowance.

2) Cut away the charm square from behind the quarter circle at least ½" away from the seam underneath.

3) Take the new cut away portion and sew it in the same manner to the top of the previous quarter circle so the block looks like one of the blocks shown above.

4) Layout the quilt as shown above.

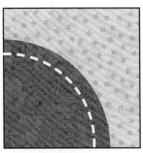

Figure A

5) Sew the blocks into rows. Sew the rows together. The quilt should now measure 36½" x 36½." Press.

6) Refer to Appendix B for instructions on sewing on borders. Take your 2½" inner border strips. First sew on the left and right borders. Then sew on the top and bottom borders. Press.

7) Take your 5½" outer border strips. First sew one onto the left and and one onto the right of the quilt. Then take the half strips and sew each of them onto a whole strip. Sew these onto the top and bottom of the quilt. Press.

8) Cut 6 -- 2½" strips width of fabric for the binding.

Bonus Quilt #2:
Charming Pinwheels
(Pinwheel Flowers without Sashing)
40" x 49"
48 Blocks
5" block (4½" finished)

While this isn't a bonus quilt at all using the definition of a bonus quilt as one made out of fabric that you already have. It is a bonus pattern, or rather an alternate setting for a previous quilt. Taking the sashing away from *Pinwheel Flowers* makes this quilt look more like the traditional pinwheel quilt. Pinwheels are a classic, much loved design. So here is a new, curved approach to the classic pinwheel.

Fabric Requirements:
72 charm (5") squares
½ yard for inner border
1 yard for outer border
1½ yards for backing
½ yard for binding

1 yard 18" wide fusible webbing

Cutting Instructions:
1) From the inner borders fabric cut 4 -- 2½" strips width of fabric:
2) From outer border fabric, cut 5 -- 5" strips width of fabric
     a) Cut one of these strips in half.

Sewing Instructions:
1) Separate charm squares into two piles: 48 background squares and 24 flower squares.

2) Using the lightweight cardboard that came with the charm squares or other template material, make a copy of the 4 inch Circle Template on page 15. Trace a 4 inch circle on the back of the 24 flower circles. Cut on the lines. Fold circles in half and finger press. Open and cut on the fold so there are 48 half circles.

3) Take the 48 background 5" squares and the 48 half circles. Place each half circle on a background square along one edge with a ¼" space as shown in **Figure A**. Press the circle in place. Repeat to make 48 blocks.

¼" space   Figure A

4) Take all 48 flower squares and topstitch, with a coordinating thread, around the curved edge with a blanket stitch, narrow zigzag, or with another decorative stitch.

5) Layout the quilt as shown above.

6) Sew the blocks into rows. Sew the rows together. The quilt should now measure 27½" x 36½." Press.

7) Take your 2½" inner border strips. First sew on the left and right borders. Then sew on the top and bottom borders. Press.

8) Take your 5½" outer border strips. First sew one onto the left and and one onto the right of the quilt. Then take the half strips and sew each of them onto a whole strip. Sew these onto the top and bottom of the quilt. Press.

9) Cut 5 -- 2½" strips width of fabric for the binding.

Appendix A: Bias Binding Tutorial

Bias binding is needed when binding a quilt with a curve anywhere along the edge. *Flowers for Sal's Table* in this book requires a bias binding because of the scalloped border. The bias of a fabric is simply the diagonal of a fabric. We cut the binding on the diagonal because it is the stretchiest part of the fabric. The stretch allows the binding to bend nicely around the curve of the quilt.

Cutting Bias Binding:

1) Open up fabric wrong side up with the selvage edges at the top and bottom.

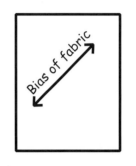
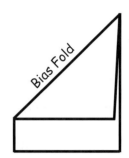

2) Take the top left corner of the fabric and fold it down to match up with the right side of the fabric.

3) Take the corner that is now at the top and fold it down to match up with the left side of the fabric.

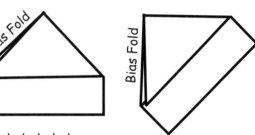
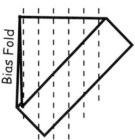

4) Rotate fabric 45° so the original bias fold is now vertical.

5) Cut off fold then cut fabric into 2½″ strips.

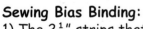

Sewing Bias Binding:

1) The 2½″ strips that were cut are all different lengths.   First sew them into one long strip at least 10″ longer than the perimeter of the quilt. These strips are sewn together with a bias seam. There are two ways to do this depending on what the edge of your strip looks like.

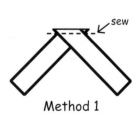

Method 1

2) Method 1: When placing your strips right sides together, some of your strips will match up nicely as shown. When this happens, simply sew the strips together as shown.

3) Method 2: If when placing your strips right sides together, they do not match up, then cut each end off square and place them at right angles to each other as shown. Sew diagonally from one corner to the other and trim off the ¼″ seam allowance as shown.

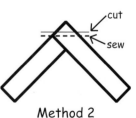

Method 2

4) Press seam allowance open.   You can also fold the binding in half lengthwise with wrong sides together and press to get it ready to sew on your quilt. Your binding is now ready to sew.

Appendix B: Midge's Perfect Borders and Sashing

Care must be taken when sewing on long pieces of fabric. This method of applying sashing and borders is perfect for the beginning (and experienced) quilter. Using this method will ensure sashing and border lay flat. They will not be too tight leaving a "pregnant" quilt, and they will not be too loose leaving borders that ripple and wave. What it does not do is ensure that a quilt is square. This method maintains the shape of the interior of the quilt. So if your blocks and rows are square and pressed neatly, this method will preserve those square angles and your entire quilt will remain square. The sewing instructions will be given for applying borders. This method also works for sewing on long sashing strips.

Preparation:

1) Press everything neatly. Press blocks that sashing will be applied to and press the entire quilt that borders will be applied to.

2) Make sure the sashing or border strips are a little longer than the blocks or quilt they are being applied to and that they are also free of creases.

3) The only tools you need are pins. Have plenty on hand.

Sewing Instructions:

1) Stand up. First we will pin the left border. Line up the top left corner of the quilt and the end of the first border strip right sides together. Pin.

2) Hold the pinned area and gently shake the quilt and the border. This allows gravity to help line up the quilt and border for a few more inches. Pin. Take care not to stretch either the quilt or the border. Continue down the border by holding the next pin, shaking out, lining up the quilt and border, and placing the next pin. Pin approximately every 8".

3) After the border is pinned, trim the border even with the end of the quilt. Take care to make this cut straight and square to prevent "dog-eared" corners.

4) Sew on border with a $\frac{1}{4}$" seam allowance. Take care not to stretch either the quilt or the border. Holding onto the pins while sewing will prevent uneven stretching. Press.

5) Repeat with the right border and then with the top and bottom borders. Generally borders are applied in this order:
   1) left and right inside borders
   2) top and bottom inside borders
   3) left and right outside borders
   4) top and bottom outside borders
If there are more borders, they are added in the same order with left and right borders generally added before top and bottom borders.

6) Viola! A few pins and standing up to let gravity help makes quick work out of long unruly borders and sashing strips.

Appendix C: Piecing a Back

Many quilt shops carry backing fabric that is 90" wide or 108" wide which is handy because it eliminates the need to piece a back for the quilt. This fabric is usually very reasonably priced. However, for many reasons, quilters often need to seam fabric together to make a back large enough for the back of a quilt.

First, when figuring out how to seam a back, be sure the back is several inches larger both in the length and the width than the quilt top. If the quilt is 40" (sometimes 42") wide or smaller, then one length of fabric will be enough. The following examples apply when the width is greater than 40". Then we need to take the length into consideration when deciding how to piece the back together.

1) **Length of the quilt is between 40" and 60"**
     ~Take the width of the fabric and round up to a nice number. That is the whole length. To find the rest of the fabric needed, take half of that amount and add it to the whole length. That is how much fabric needs to be purchased.
     ~Cut the fabric into 2 pieces--one piece will be the "whole" length and the second piece will be the "half" length. Take the "half" length and cut it in half lengthwise. Lengthwise is the long side that is parallel to the selvedge. This cut will often be made on or close to the fold put in the fabric by the manufacturer.
     ~Sew the two short sides of this "half" length together so that now it is as long as the "whole" length. Sew onto the two lengths together as shown in Figure A.

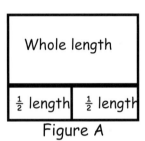
Figure A

2) **Length of the quilt is between 60" and 80"**
     ~Most of the quilts in this book require this type of seaming. It is also the quickest.
     ~Take the width of the fabric and round up to a nice number. That is the whole length.
     ~Two lengths are need so the amount is doubled. That is how much fabric needs to be purchased.
     ~Cut the fabric in half so there are two "whole" lengths.
     Sew the two lengths together along the selvedge as shown in Figure B.

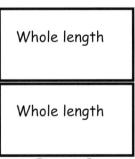
Figure B

3) **Length of the quilt is between 80" and 100"**
     ~Take the width of the fabric and round up to a nice number. That is the whole length. To find the rest of the fabric needed, take half of that amount and add it to TWO whole lengths. That is how much fabric needs to be purchased.
     ~Cut the fabric into two "whole" lengths and one "half" length.
     ~Take the "half" length and cut it in half lengthwise. Lengthwise is the long side that is parallel to the selvedge. This cut will often be made on or close to the fold put in the fabric by the manufacturer.
     ~Sew the two short sides of this "half" length together so that now it is as long as the "whole" length. Sew onto the three lengths together as shown in Figure C.

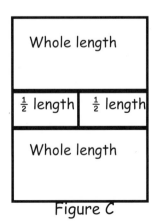
Figure C